GW00360691

ACKNOWLEDGEMENTS F'

The Chairman and members of the Shere, Go........ .... Society are grateful to Dr. Peter Brandon, Head of the Department of Geography, The Polytechnic of North London, for writing this booklet and also to his colleagues in the same Department, Claire Wastie for her sketches and photographs and Robin Skinner for general help.

The author wishes to express gratitude to Dr. Mason and Mrs. Wells, Librarian and Hon. Archivist respectively of Christ Church College, Oxford and to Mrs. Shirley Corke, Archivist, Surrey County Council, the custodians of most of the documentary evidence for the changing human landscape of the Tillingbourne Valley which has been used in this booklet.

Thanks are also due to Professor Alan and Mrs. Glenys Crocker who have been unstinting in sharing their knowledge of the Surrey paper industry and of the Chilworth gunpowder sites. To landowners thanks are also cordially expressed for permission to visit sites on private property.

Acknowledgement is made to the British Museum for permission to reproduce the illustration on page 27 and to Christ Church College, Oxford for similar permission to reproduce the illustrations on pages 11 & 12.

Responsibility for all statements rests with the author.

By 2003 some people mentioned above have retired from the positions quoted.

Thanks are due to the committee & Ronny Karlsson for his technical expertise for the 2003 reprint.

ISBN 0-9550620-2-0

Published by the Shere, Gomshall & Peaslake Local History Society
All rights reserved
1984
Reprinted 1996
Revised and Reprinted 1998
Revised and Reprinted 2003
Reprinted 2006
Reprinted 2010

Jamaica Press 2010

USING THE BOOKLET

The water-milling and other sites connected with the manipulation of water referred to in this booklet are enumerated in the order of their location along the short length of the Tillingbourne from its sources on the flanks of Leith Hill above Wotton, past Shere, Albury and Chilworth to its confluence with the river Wey at Shalford near Guildford. The location of each site is given by means of a Grid Reference of six digits (a unique reference system which is explained on all Ordnance Survey topographical maps). For each site brief details are given of the visible features and its history.

All the sites mentioned can be closely approached by means of public roads, footpaths and bridle-ways but almost all lie on private property and it may not be practicable for landowners to grant permission to visit the sites themselves except by special arrangement, in which case application should be made well in advance of an intended visit, and preferably by letter. Readers are asked to take particular care in the closing of field gates and avoidance of litter and not to trespass on private property in the course of their walks.

It is impossible in a work of this kind to supply the references in support of statements made. Readers who wish to study this corroborative evidence for themselves will find some of it set out in other works by the author, viz:

"Land, technology and water management in the Tillingbourne valley, Surrey, 1560-1760", *Southern History Vol. 6* 1984.

"An early conversion of 'prospect' into 'landscape': Sir John Evelyn at Wotton, Surrey".

Supplementing the landscape approach of this booklet in many ways is J.Hillier's classic *Old Surrey water-mills* (1952) which although often inaccurate in historical fact is an invaluable account of the old craft of milling, its buildings and machinery.

Paddington Farmhouse (see page 22)

INTRODUCING THE WATER FEATURES OF THE TILLINGBOURNE VALLEY

This little essay is written for the many people who delight in exploring the beautiful valley of the Tillingbourne between Dorking and Guildford, and especially those who have felt the charm of water-mills, both working and deserted. Its aim is to demonstrate human ingenuity in the art of exploiting water as a resource in a district so long favoured and settled that waters have been gathered to curve on the breast of overshot water-wheels not uncommonly spread out at intervals of less than a half mile. Thanks largely to the crucial protection against despoliation by building in the 1930s afforded by its leading landowners, the valley of the Tillingbourne is neither Metroland nor suburbia but a still recognizable part of the Surrey scene which has descended to us from John Aubrey's seventeenth-century 'little romancy vale' and Williams Cobbett's 'one of the choices retreats of man'. Its scenery in fact is as beautiful of its kind as any in England but it is easy to forget that this beauty is not entirely natural. Half of its beauty is due to the conscious and unconscious manipulation of water which has given the valley an incomparable legacy of varied water features created by the diversion and gathering of streams and the building of dams.

To this end this booklet is about the millers who dammed streams and made mill-ponds; industrialists who manufactured goods with the aid of water-driven machinery of increasing mechanical efficiency; landscape gardeners who adopted the technique of the miller in making canal water-gardens; farmers who periodically watered meadows by the process known as floating; and the others who combined to create a valley meshed by water channelled and dammed. By way of background, something is also said of the foresters who in hewing the wood fuel to feed the industrial mills unwittingly changed the visual appearance of the valley into something resembling its present-day aspect.

The essay is therefore a study in the field of landscape history, a still relatively new approach pioneered and popularized by Professor W.G. Hoskins in which archaeology, history, geography and ecology meet. The ultimate aim of this approach is to retrieve, record, analyse and interpret the neglected evidence imprinted on the ground itself so that, in conjunction with written evidence, we can understand better the human societies and productive forces that helped to evolve the present landscape. Even if the mill has vanished to its foundations the pond still remains to be located and the dry leat traced back to its union with the main stream.

THE TILLINGBOURNE VALLEY AND ITS WATER TECHNOLOGY

The Tillingbourne, only some eleven miles in length, rises in strong springs on the northern flanks of Leith Hill, the highest point in southern England, and flows through a fertile valley lying between two ranges of diversified soft hills, the North Downs and the sandstones developed on the Lower Greensand formation. It is still easy today to recall the country gentlemen and their families who long lived classically at ease in the quiet, placid countryside of their choice – the Malthuses, Barclays, Evelyns, Brays, Morgans and Randalls, mostly originating as *arriviste* Tudor gentry in succession to long-established medieval families such as the Westons of Albury. A number of them were of outstanding distinction and entered into the national life of England, amongst them being Sir Reginald Bray of Shere, a senior minister of Henry VII and designer of the Henry VII chapels of Westminster and Windsor; John Evelyn of Wotton, the prolific diarist and author of *Sylva* (1664), the first book in English devoted to forestry; and Thomas Robert Malthus of Westcott, author of the famous *Essay on the Principle of Population* (1798).

Abinger mill

It is much less easy to visualize the time when the quietude of the valley was periodically shattered by gunpowder blasts or to think of it when the lower course of the river stank with the effluent of paper mills and the hillsides were stripped and sterile, providing a living for fewer people on the land than formerly. In the early middle ages the tamed powers of the Tillingbourne worked corn mills and fulling mills. The latter prepared cloth in advance of dyeing and were introduced from the fourteenth century. In the sixteenth and seventeenth centuries the use of the water-wheel greatly expanded again and the Tillingbourne acquired a new importance as a source of energy for driving trip-hammers for iron, brass and wire manufacture and also wheels for the making of gunpowder, saw-milling, paper-manufacture and knife-grinding. Other water-using industries also gravitated to the river, notably leather-tanning. In addition to the other economic uses to which the regulated river was put, the floating of meadows for the sake of rich fresh grass in the spring was a conspicuous example. Ornamental canals, serpentined rivers, cascades and waterfalls were applied to garden layouts with the same skilful engineering techniques initially acquired in the industrial management of water. In the nineteenth century the main products of the valley's mills were gunpowder and bank-notes, the former being manufactured at Chilworth until well within living memory. There can scarcely be in England a valley richer in historical associations of the developing art of directing sources of power in nature for the use and convenience of man. Contemporaries were themselves aware that they had created a sharply differentiated landscape.

The diarist John Evelyn himself observed of it in1675: "I do not remember to have seen such a variety of mills and works upon so narrow a brook and in so little a compass: there being mills for corn, cloth, brass, iron, powder, etc.." Earlier still, the cartographer John Norden had supplied proof of the intensification of milling in the Tillingbourne valley by distinguishing on his map of Surrey (1594) a cluster of five water-mills on the short stretch of the river upstream of Gomshall alone, the largest single concentration of mills depicted in a small area on any of his county maps.

Human ingenuity in the manipulation of water-power was gradually perfected in the Tillingbourne valley by its leading landowners. A number of these were right at the heart of 'projecting', as industrial development was termed in the seventeenth century

4

and hence closely involved with new contrivances worked by water. Foremost in the art of managing the waters were the Evelyns of Wotton. The diarist's grandfather,

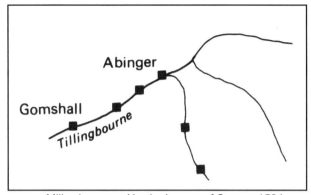

Mills shown on Norden's map of Surrey, 1594.

George Evelyn, bought the Wotton estate in 1579 when the earlier disparking of Abinger Park and rich store of woodland on the commons of Wotton and Abinger made it 'ripe' for industrial development. His youngest son Richard who succeeded him at Wotton in 1603 was remembered in family tradition as a 'thriving, neat, silent and methodical genius'. During his ownership of Wotton until 1641 his father's role in gunpowder manufacture was diversified into brass, wire and iron to compensate for the family's loss of the gunpowder monopoly. His son, John, the diarist, owed much to his father's conserving instincts and inherited some of his practical aptitudes. His tastes were towards re-afforestation of lands which his forebears had stripped bare and his special contribution to the Tillingbourne valley was garden landscapes. His aptness in handling water for canal-water gardens at Wotton and Albury was as he himself boasted "one of the first examples of that elegancy since so much in vogue".

Although the Evelyns were the most ambitious of the local 'projectors' they were by no means the sole source of water-power technology in the Tillingbourne valley. The Hills of Abinger, the Morgans and Randalls of Chilworth, the Brays of Shere and the Le Steeres of Wotton and Ockley were also energetic participators in industrial ventures. Apart from the Le Steeres, an old landed family in the area, the others had migrated to the valley for the sake of the opportunities it offered to the enterprising industrialist. By their efforts the valley was turned into an important rural workshop, famed for its inventiveness.

The catching of the river water for power at the mill and the use of the river water for industrial processing was more and more widely extended to bring in new industries which in turn replaced the old. The expanding agricultural economy of the late 16th and the early 17th centuries should not be overlooked, for this had a great effect on the scale and intensity of milling. The floating of water-meadows, denshiring barren land, the introduction of up-and-down husbandry and new crops and grasses were enormously important innovations in Surrey because the county had a great reservoir of poor to average land which was economically marginal or sub-marginal. As more and more new land was taken into cultivation so more water was harnessed for milling corn. This took several forms; many mills which originally worked only one pair of stones became multiple mills, thus greatly extending their capacity. New sources of power were tapped between the medieval mills and higher up the water courses to serve new fields and communities.

This agricultural expansion can be most clearly worked out on the three estates of the Evelyns of Wotton, the Brays of Shere and the Steeres of Ockley. Substantial acreages of the North Downs crest and the sandy soils of the Leith Hill district were denshired and brought under the plough between 1560 and about 1640. This process has brought into being a characteristic pattern of uniformly square or rectangular fields, typically bounded by low earthbanks and quickset hedges, and sporadic small farms such as can be readily seen at Abinger Bottom and Broadmoor. Milling continued into the early nineteenth century and lingered on until the First World War. Other forms of milling had shorter histories. The first of the industrial forms of milling to become obsolete was the fulling of cloth. This decayed with the decline of the cloth industry centred upon Guildford and Godalming in the early seventeenth century and fulling sites were taken over for gunpowder and iron manufacture. Iron in its turn also decayed, the famous forge at Abinger Hammer operating until the last quarter of the eighteenth century. By then the most vigorous milling activity was that of paper making which with the gunpowder works at Chilworth represented the characteristic industry in the early nineteenth century. From the late nineteenth century onwards the old milling sites have been adapted to other purposes, notably water-cress and trout farms, light engineering factories and laboratories and delightful picturesque gardens.

The application of water power in the past is therefore still strongly influencing land use long after it has been discontinued. Many mill-ponds, although 'dry' are too waterlogged for farming purposes and contain a rich store of tangled woodland which greatly diversifies the valley. This survival of traditional rural culture is one of the great differentiating strengths of the valley at the present time which it is hoped sympathetic planning will continue far into the future.

Though so short in length, the Tillingbourne was thus of great importance to Surrey agriculture and to the county's manufacturers before the Industrial Revolution robbed it of its trades. Its swift waters flowing down a relatively steep gradient and in a narrow, often ravine-like valley, lent itself to damming up to form a staircase of ponds. Much of the heavy rain that falls on its hillsides sinks through the porous rocks of the chalk and sandstone and gives rise to numerous springs breaking out at the valley sides.

These springs sufficiently augmented the flow in summer to provide at all times an adequate flow of water for all-the-year round working and the mills were rarely prevented by an overflow or impeded by frost. The small risk of flooding in past times is clearly indicated in the valley by the sites of mills and other buildings close to the river banks, as in the village of Shere. Of the local springs, the most powerful single feeder of the Tillingbourne is the Sherbourne (formerly Shireburn) Spring, which forms the Silent

Pool at Albury. From the sixteenth to the eighteenth centuries this was the most fiercely contested natural resource in the whole of the Tillingbourne valley, being used for a number of conflicting purposes, including milling of paper and gunpowder at Chilworth and Albury, the floating of water meadows at Weston and to supply the water fountains at the once magnificent garden of Albury.

George Cole, *The Tillingbourne near Albury* (c.1850)

PLACES

The first group of water-milling sites and other places connected in various ways with the harnessing of water lies in the parishes of Wotton and Abinger. In these parishes the old craft of milling by water-power has its own particular distinctiveness. The sixteenth and early seventeenth-century mills were mainly industrial and of the type which requires relatively small amounts of water-power in the processing of manufactured goods. Gunpowder, brass and wire were characteristic of these industries. These were particularly suited to the headwaters of the Tillingbourne not only on account of the limited water supplies in the upper course of the river but also the comparative remoteness which offered greater safety in the working of gunpowder. The most powerful factor actuating this industrial development in the early modern period was, however, the extensive woodland available to feed the mills. The first step taken to open up the district to industrial use was in 1464 when the park of Abinger which spread widely across both Wotton and Abinger parishes was disparked. This invited speculative development long before George Evelyn purchased the manor of Wotton in 1579. It particularly attracted immigrant Tudor gentry of a Welsh origin who were amongst the strongest supporters of Henry VII, such as David Owen of Wotton, the Morgans of Chilworth and Abinger, the Brays of Shere and also Richard Hill of Chilworth and Abinger. These were the first developers of the industrial potential of the two parishes.

By a series of shrewd investments these lands and mills were gathered together into the possession of the family of Evelyn of Wotton: the ancient manor of Wotton was bought by George Evelyn in 1579; his son Richard added the manor of Abinger in 1622, the manor of Paddington in Abinger in 1625, Westcott manor in 1628, the iron forge at Abinger Hammer in 1631 and Gosterwood in 1636. The woods on the common of the Manwood, stretching for over 900 acres over the northern flanks of Leith Hill and common to both tenants of Wotton and Abinger were the richest prize of these manors in the mid-sixteenth century. Great quantities of wood were felled and burnt in the manufacture of gunpowder, brass and iron. Such activities brought the need of larger numbers of tenants or labourers and this in turn required the improvement of land for small-holdings.

1. Brookmill NGR.TQ139455   *Impressive pond-bays; drained ponds; ponds and leat supplying ornamental cascade.*

This is likely to be one of the three water-mill sites recorded on John Norden's map of Surrey (1594), the others probably being Friday Street and Wotton. Speed's augmented

map of Norden's (1605-10) shows the same information. Brookmill is closely identified with George Evelyn, the gunpowder manufacturer, who enclosed Brookwick Coppice (lying adjacent to the west) from the extensive Manwood Common covering most of Wotton and Abinger about 1584. The bounds of this coppice can still be traced by means of the boundary bank and ditch thrown up at the time of the enclosure. A little earlier, New Coppice had been enclosed by Edmund Hill, lord of the manor of Abinger. This enclosure extends along the track leading to Leith Hill which passes by the Brookmill site and runs across towards Friday Street; it can again be identified by its boundary banks. Coppiced timber in this enclosure supplied the iron mill at Abinger Hammer with fuel.

The purpose of Evelyn's Brookwick enclosure was also doubtless to provide fuel for the mill at Brookmill. Possibly a store

Richard Redgrave,
Evelyn woods near Friday Street (c.1856)

of alder for gunpowder making was raised here for the site had been so miry and remote from settlement that it was argued in defence of the enclosure that local inhabitants had not previously endangered themselves and their animals by using that part of the common for pasture or fuel supplies. Evidence given in 1609 in connection with a dispute involving the enclosure refers to "six new cottages and a mill" erected on the common of the Manwood within the previous thirty years. This statement appears to refer to the millsite of Brookmill and to the origin of the present hamlet of Broadmoor which thus probably owes its existence to the advent of late sixteenth-century milling.

2. Ornamental cascade NGR.TQ138458

Water-filled leat contouring on high ground; four-stepped cascade.

The ornamental cascade

A contour leat, still containing water, leads off from Brookmill Pond and can be followed across rough land to a point some four hundred yards south-west, whence it continues through private grounds to supply the cascade. These features were constructed c.1738 by a retired Dutchman, Mr. Jacobsen, as a set piece of an illustrious early eighteenth-century garden landscape centred upon the present cottage and walled gardens lying adjacent to the north.

From late eighteenth century descriptions, it is apparent that numerous small islands in the river were clumped with firs and on one a Gothic pavilion was erected. The adjoining meadows were adorned with lead vases and stone statues. Numerous ornamental basins and 'jets d'eau' diversified the grounds around the house. The hilltop overlooking the house was crowned with Cedars of Lebanon and beautiful plantations of oak and fir spread outwards to complete a noble picture around the eighty-foot cascade.

3. Wotton Meads NGR. TQ125065

Ornamental cascade and series of dams of small head occupying a mile-long meadow and in almost regular order.

The adjacent drawing shows part of the landscaping of Sir John Evelyn, grandson of the diarist John Evelyn, who resided at Wotton House between 1706 and 1763. His 'new river' is one of the earliest projects in 'serpenting' in the country and remains substantially unaltered since construction between c.1736 and 1740, rather earlier than William Kent's mature work at Rousham, Oxon. There is the possibility that Evelyn was influenced in the matter of these water features by his visit to Castle Howard, Yorkshire, where he observed a serpentine river under construction for the Earl of Carlisle. Other visits to country seats in the 1730s reveal how attentive Sir John Evelyn was to canals, rivers and cascades, with the apparent aim of adopting some of the principles of construction himself and avoiding what he regarded as imperfections.

Wotton meads, showing fishponds constructed by Sir John Evelyn

4. Fountain leat NGR. TQ125465   *Leat supplying water to the*
fountain in the temple garden
of Wotton.

This leat, which is still in working order, was constructed by the diarist John Evelyn with the aid of his brother George and cousin Captain Evelyn, c.1652, to supply water to the fountain in the temple of the newly constructed garden at Wotton House. The leat is drawn off from a point about fifty feet higher than the floor of the upper of a fine flight of terraces constructed by the Evelyns and supplies the fountain and circular basin by gravity. It is characteristic of John Evelyn that his practical skills in applied hydraulics were employed in re-modelling landscape in the manner he had observed in Italy when on a Grand Tour, and which he was later to apply to Albury. There is also the possibility that John Evelyn advised the Randalls on the similar garden-making at Chilworth, further down-stream. Evelyn's work at Wotton was to make it one of the most splendid and best-known of the mid-seventeenth century Italianate canal-water gardens.

George Scharf, *View of Dorking* (1823)

Evelyn's work was to make the Tillingbourne flow over an artificially constructed cascade below the hamlet of Friday Street and through a chain of fishponds each divided by a small cascade. The work involved enlarging the bed of the stream through sheets of gravel and cutting a river course in a more irregular manner. The gradient of the stream was also steepened by raising the cascade at the upper end. A merit of the work is the fastidious attention given to the brick-and stone-work. The latter was obtained from Westcott Heath. The bordering walks were planted with willow and other suitable native trees.

The painting by George Lambert (1739) realistically records the 'New River' tumbling over low falls in the foreground, the absence of walls and fences and cattle-grazed meadows. The present scene has altered very little since Sir John's day. This landscaping is an interesting example of that of the generation which bridged the gap between classical and romantic attitudes in landscape. Sir John Evelyn's re-adornment of John Evelyn's birthplace with economically profitable forestry covering the flanks of the Tillingbourne valley was a fortunate opportunity for him to work out some ambitious ideas in the new relationship between open countryside and the strict formality of the enclosed garden of early Hanoverian England

George Lambert, *Wotton Park, 1739*. Notice the mill-pond on the right.

5. Friday Street NGR. TQ128458

Pond-bay, mill-pond, mill-house, enclosures for coppiced and ornamental trees.

This old mill-pond has long been a favourite rendezvous of Surrey trippers but, strangely, little has been written of its history. It lies remote from the settlements of Wotton and the Abingers on the water-parting of the two parishes. Hillier suggests that the mill here was that recorded at Wotton in Domesday. This is incorrect. The damming of the stream and the making of the lake occurred in the late sixteenth century. The precise date is unknown for the clues as to the origin of the mill here are only to be found in the depositions of witnesses before an Examiner of the Court of Chancery which reflected a continuing, if intermittent, struggle of tenants of the manors of Wotton and Abinger to oppose the enclosure of the part of the Manwood Common known as the New Coppice and the Brookwick Copse.

According to Richard Evelyn, one of the witnesses called before the Court in 1609 the mill was then a corn mill which had been built years before it came into his hands. A deed of 1616 helps to pin-point its origin more exactly by describing the site as a "watermill, millhouse, wheels, millstones lately erected on Wotton common, together with floodgates,

Richard Redgrave,
Near Friday Street (c.1850)

sluices and mill ponds". Another witness's statement in Chancery was to the effect that the mill had been erected within the thirty years previous to 1609. The mill at Friday Street thus almost certainly owes it origin to George Evelyn who bought Wotton manor in 1579. It is conceivable that Richard Hill, joint lord of Abinger and Wotton manors, who enclosed the four-hundred acre New Coppice a little earlier, may have been responsible for the mill as well. Although in use as a corn mill in 1604, it may possibly have begun its history as a gunpowder mill. Another possible powdermill of early origin is some five hundred yards up-stream (Site 6). Apart from the millhouse, which still survives, Richard Evelyn permitted two cottages to be erected on the waste at Friday Street: this marks the beginning of the mill-hamlet itself, which lies attractively on the southern edge of the mill-pond.

Hugh Browne was miller in 1604. The mill was later known as Noones, presumably the name of an early-seventeenth century miller. In William Holliday's tenure in the mid-seventeenth century the mill comprised two corn mills under the same roof, one a wheat mill and the other a malt mill. Even at this early date, only one mill-pond was in use: the one at Site 2 had even then apparently been drained, which is strongly suggestive that this was one of George Evelyn's powder-making sites. The timbered portion of the cottage lying below the mill dam is possibly part of the old mill.

The Friday Street mills were closed down by their owner, Sir John Evelyn c. 1736, who transferred his tenant to Elwix Mill in Abinger (Site 9), then no longer being used as an industrial site. Ever since the mill-pond has been retained for ornamental purposes. The mill-pond, without the mill, is shown on Rocque's map of Surrey (1768). Evelyn's closure of the mill is an early example of the changing taste which was transforming parts of Surrey from working scenes to the broader scale of landscape. Sir John Evelyn, like his grandfather, the diarist John Evelyn, was essentially a planter whose main distinction lay in the woods with which he re-clothed the slopes of the Tillingbourne valley. Although primarily concerned with economically profitable forestry he landscaped on a heroic scale the outlying parts of his great estate in the manner of Stephen Switzer's 'rural, extensive and forest gardening'. The cardinal principle of Switzer's (as of Alexander Pope's circle, with which Sir John Evelyn was connected by his sister's marriage) was the practice of gardening, at once picturesque and utilitarian.

These principles Evelyn applied to the Tillingbourne downstream from the old mill at Friday Street. Two considerations led to the closure of the mill, both aesthetic ones. Firstly, he had determined to enlarge the channel and steepen the gradient of the Tillingbourne, 'serpenting' it in the process in order to create the chain of fishponds separated by low falls which still survive below the artificial waterfall at NGR TQ127460. The stretches of water between the falls were known as 'canals'. Secondly, he chose to plant specimen trees on the natural bluff overlooking the mill-pond to the east of the cottage of half-timber construction which was the old millhouse. This was part of Evelyn's overall landscaping of his estate and the site was chosen partly for the reason that from the top of the bluff a view was then afforded of St. Paul's some twenty four miles away.

John Clayton Adams, *A wooded river valley (Abinger Hammer meadows)* (c.1885)

Since the early nineteenth century, Friday Street has been famed for its picturesque qualities. John Varley, one of the first realist watercolourists, painted at Friday Street c.1806 and Richard Redgrave (who painted in the area for thirty-six years and is commemorated by a plaque in Abinger church), J.C. Hook and William Rose spent a season there in 1853. Ball's painting of 1908, used for the accompanying drawing, is of interest in its record of the growth of trees and scrub around the waterside since the end of common grazing.

14

6. Pond-bay NGR. TQ128453   *Pond-bay; outline of pond visible.*

As the natural flow of the upper course of the Tillingbourne was so small it was necessary to impound water above the milling heads to ensure an adequate supply. This pond-bay marks one such site. The pond was possibly worked in connection with the Friday Street mill-site but some connection with gunpowder making is possible. It is presumably to sites such as this that the diarist John Evelyn was referring when c.1675 he stated that "not far from my brother's house (at Wotton) upon the streams and ponds since filled up and drained, stood formerly many powder-mills, erected by my ancestors…" He also refers to an explosion at one of these nearby powdermills which damaged Wotton House.

7. Pigeon House pond site,   *Pond-bay.*
   Wotton House NGR. TQ120470

This is the site of the Wotton wire mills owned by Richard Evelyn and rented by Peter Brocklesby, a London pewterer from 1627 to an indeterminate date, probably in the late 1640s. A lease of the wire mills to Brocklesby in 1644 refers to the works as 'brass or wyre works' with an adjacent orchard garden 'at or near the Pondhead or Bay of that pond called the Pigeon House pond'. Provision was made in the lease for George Evelyn (the diarist's brother) to store fish in the pond and for him to 'stop up and make firm as much of the said pond as he thinks fit for the enlarging and increasing of any buildings, ways and passages near his new dwelling house, stable and out-house and Pigeon house'. The wire mills were leased to Joseph Mulford in 1625 and to William Cowes, als. Standish in 1627.

These works were a successful attempt to infringe the monopoly of the Mineral and Battery Company's brass-plate and wire-drawing operations. Another similar works was erected at Abinger or Elwix Mill (Site 9). The Wotton works comprised both a copper mill and a wire-works. At the copper mill, the imported copper ingots would have been treated with calamine stone to introduce zinc for making into brass. The wire-works would then have turned the brass into wire-goods such as lattice-work for windows, chains, fish-hooks, pack-needles and rings for curtains. John Evelyn refers to a water-driven 'enginio' obtained from Sweden for this purpose. This was a great advance on the primitive method of hand-made wire earlier adopted in England and was probably similar in operation to the seventeenth-century machine described by John Ray, which involved a water driven axle-tree operating pairs of pincers alternately opening and shutting against a drawing plate.

In John Evelyn's sketch of Wotton house in 1652 can be identified the pigeon house, the pigeon house pond and buildings on the west bank of the pond which probably represent the site of the wire works of Peter Brocklesby. By 1675, the Wotton wire works had been removed farther from the house as part of the Evelyn brothers' landscaping and building projects.

Brocklesby, who also made brass goods at Abinger or Elwix Mill for a brief period (Site 9), apparently first manufactured them under a privilege granted by the Mineral and Battery Company but was alleged to have violated its conditions and thereafter engaged in persistent defiance of its monopoly. Lawyers engaged by the Crown to arbitrate between the two parties reported Brocklesby as 'obstinate and wilful' and a man who has had 'no breeding or hath any skill (in brass manufacture) being himself now a pewterer and keeping a pewterer's shop using only strangers, (i.e. foreigners) in his employment'. The London pewterer did not contest this description but by 1639, at which date his opposition to the company from Wotton had extended over more than twelve years, he claimed to be able to undersell the Mineral and Battery Company's products by a wide margin and that the foreigners he had introduced at great expense had taught the craft of wire-making to Englishmen. Nevertheless, his output remained small for he was unable to export his products to the rich markets of the Guinea Coast and the Indies, which was the right of the monopolists.

Brocklesby's lease of 1644 throws interesting incidental light on George Evelyn's building operations at Wotton. The 'new dwelling house' completed by that date is shown by another of John Evelyn's sketches to have taken the form of a large house with two opposing wings, east and west. The part-draining of the pond at some date between 1644 and 1675 suggests that George Evelyn built further buildings on the site of the old wire works. The house was further altered by Sir John Evelyn c.1715-18 and extensively by Sir Frederick Evelyn in the mid-nineteenth century.

John Evelyn's sketch c.1652 of Pigeon House pond
(in foreground) and buildings which had probably been
used as a wire-works.

16

8. NGR. TQ129118   *Faint trace of a levelled
                               platform.*

A levelled platform, probably raised to carry an oblong timber building, is visible on the left bank of the river, set with its long axis parallel to the stream. This site could represent a site of buildings used in connection with Brocklesby's wire-works

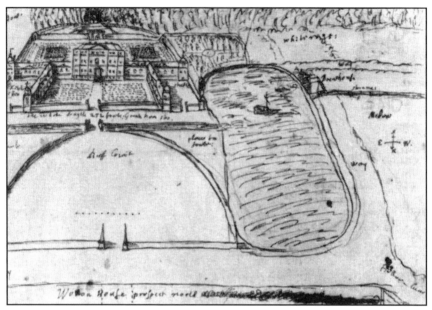

John Evelyn's sketch-plan of Wotton House, gardens, mill-pond.
The brewhouse is on or near the former site of wire-works.

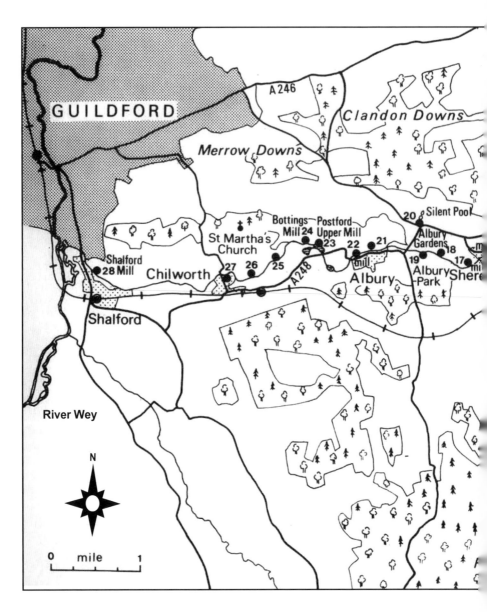

The numbered sites on this location map correspond to numbers in the text. Based, with permission, on the Ordnance Survey 1:50,000 map

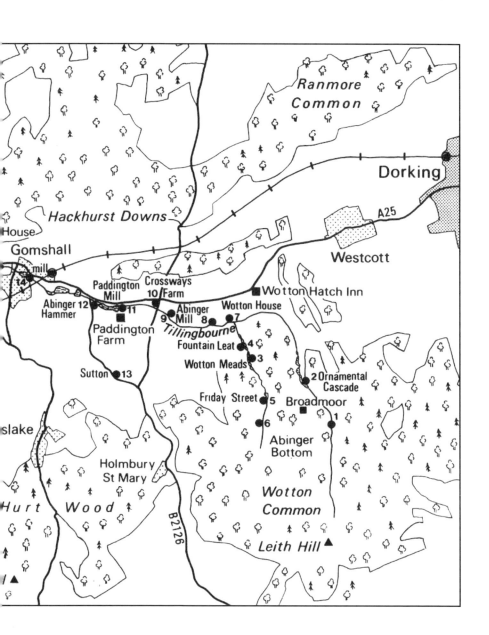

Ranmore Common

Dorking

A25

Hackhurst Downs

House

Gomshall

Westcott

mill

14

Paddington Mill

Crossways Farm 10

Wotton Hatch Inn

Abinger 12 Hammer

11

Abinger Mill 9

8

Wotton House

Paddington Farm

Tillingbourne

7

Fountain Leat 4

Wotton Meads 3

Sutton 13

2 Ornamental Cascade

Friday Street 5

Broadmoor

1

slake

6

Abinger Bottom

Holmbury St Mary

Wotton Common

Hurt Wood

B2126

Leith Hill

9. Abinger Mill   NGR. TQ110460

Pond-bay; drained pond;
mill-house; picturesque garden.

This is a fine example of the site of a multiple mill converted in the seventeenth century from a small corn mill probably existing before 1086. It was know variously as Yelwicke, Elwix, Abinger and Crane's mill.

It is recorded as a gunpowder mill owned by Richard Hill, lord of the manor of Abinger and a partner of George Evelyn in powder-making. At the end of the sixteenth century, part of the manor became the property of William Morgan of Chilworth who leased the mills to George Bromell, a local man. A reference to the 'powder bay' at Elwix mill in 1622 suggests that powder-making was still in continuance or only recently ended. In the same year, Richard Evelyn partly converted the mills to a copper mill, tenanted by Henry Deane who was followed by Peter Brocklesby. Deane used the mill as a 'batter' mill, i.e. producing brass and copper plate not for wire but for consumer goods such as pans, kettles, ladles, etc., as well as for receptacles needed for gunpowder manufacture. A deed of 1667 describes the site as "one corn mill and the other now, or lately, a coppermill, heretofore a powdermill". In 1670, it was further enlarged and working three water-mills under one roof, one for grinding wheat, one for malt and the other for oats. It survived as a corn mill until the end of the nineteenth century. Richard Redgrave, Frank Walton and many other late Victorian landscape artists have painted Abinger Mill.

Abinger mill garden.

10. Floated water-meadows, NGR. TQ107471
Crossways Farm

Parallel leats across fields attached to fine seventeenth century farmhouse.

The fields bear traces of a series of parallel leats intended to cover them with a skilfully managed sheet of running water, about one inch deep, flowing continuously over the water meadows for the sake of the 'feed' of grass in spring or the enlarged hay crop produced by the fertilizing properties of the system of 'floating'. By a deed of 1622, William Leigh sold to Richard Evelyn a parcel of land bordering the pond bay of Elwix mill, doubtless for an extension to the millpond, and in return gained the right to make a trench through Evelyn's land for the purpose of taking one half of the Tillingbourne water on Sundays and Holy days during the months of April and May, the most critical season for watering meadows. This arrangement explains how 'floating' and the many other uses of mill water could be integrated without conflict. A similar system of leats for 'floating' is observable at Abinger Hammer (site 12).

John Clayton Adams, *Paddington mill-pond* (1886)

21

11. Paddington mill NGR. TQ101471

Small nineteenth-century mill; drained pond; fine old farmhouse and barns at Paddington farm.

A mill existed on this site before 1086. In the early fourteenth century, Roger de Jarpenville granted to Gilbert the Fuller a fulling mill here, together with a mill-pond, water-course, fishery, two messuages and a garden. This presumably represents an extension of the milling carried on at Paddington. The present brick building bears the inscription 'W.J. Evelyn 1867' and the name of Thomas Spencer, millwright of Guildford, is recorded on the iron pentrough. The building is now disused and most traces of the iron overshot wheel, visible forty years ago, have disappeared.

12. Abinger Forge mill NGR. TQ095475

Modern factory on site; traces of masonry for sluice gate.

This iron forge was one of the most famous in the Weald on account of Richard Elrington's special exemption from restriction on fuel-cutting within the area of London. It was commonly known in the sixteenth century as Shere forge because of its connection with the Brays of Shere. The name 'Paddington forge' also occurs in the seventeenth century and its forgemen as 'ironmen of Paddingdoune'. Elrington tenanted the iron mill from Edmund Bray and in 1549, it is stated that he had 'newe defaced in the stede and place' of a pre-existing water-mill, 'an iron-hammer and mill or forge'. Edmund Bray contracted to supply him with iron sows of bar iron from his furnace at Vachery in Cranleigh. It was the creation of this forge which led to the enclosure of New Coppice, some 400 acres in all, and also Heathy land, both high-lying parts of the former common of the Manwood. Tenants uprooted fences around the New Coppice towards the end of the sixteenth century but the lord of the manor subsequently re-erected them. The final decision of the Court of Chancery was in favour of the new owner of the forge, Jane Browker, on the grounds that the enclosures had been taken out of the common with the consent of almost all the tenants. Besides taking cordwood from the enclosed parcels of the Manwood, she was entitled to cut 3000 loads annually from the unenclosed common. In 1588, the production of the forge may have fallen, for its consumption of fuelwood was estimated at 2400 loads annually.

The forge came into possession of Jane's son, Thomas Browker, in the early seventeenth century, who negotiated its sale to Richard Evelyn over a period of more than six years. Browker's initial selling price for the forge and its woods was £2200 in 1626. Evelyn evidently considered this on the high side and drew attention to the fact that "these parts of the country are already full of mills" and that as the mill was not on a navigable waterway it was less valuable. Evelyn's offer of £1500 was finally accepted in 1631. Evelyn rented the mill as an iron forge to Francis Pellat, who paid £40 per annum, the same sum as Evelyn had earned from powdermills prior to their removal.

It is easy to read between the lines of the correspondence between Browker and Evelyn to realize that the profitability of a forge depended upon a convenient supply of bar iron not too far distant from navigable water. The Abinger hammer suffered from inaccessibility. The use of imported Spanish and Swedish bar iron made matters worse in this respect. At the beginning of the eighteenth century, the rent was halved to £20 per annum and the tenant, John Dibble, who had to contend with cheap imported iron at that period, was a poor manager. The closing phase of the iron mill takes the form of a tragi-comedy. In the 1720's, Dibble had bad relations with his workers. On one occasion, his men refused to work with him and his foreman went to work at another forge in Sussex. Even his son admitted that any association with him at the forge was impossible. Partly through his mismanagement, Dibble incurred heavy arrears of rent and his plan to pay off his debts by marrying a local widow was unsuccessful. Eventually his goods were distrained and Sir John Evelyn secured possession of the mill.

Sir Frederick Evelyn made several attempts to revive the mill when its iron-making career came to end about 1788. He aimed to re-introduce gunpowder manufacture, but local opposition precluded this. He was also prepared to let it as a corn mill, claiming that "more corn may be ground here than at any other mill between Dorking and Shalford, it being supplied with water sufficient to drive two overshot wheels with force enough to work two pairs of stones each". A paper or fulling mill were also considered practicable. In the event, these plans came to nought and it was the even better site of Gomshall mill, well served by a railway station, that was to become the key corn milling site.

13. Sutton   NGR. TQ100460

Pond-bay; mill-house; drained pond.

In the fourteenth century, a fulling mill existed here, the wooded slopes of the valley being called Fulvenshanger. Probably a manorial corn mill was also working at the same time.

From Abinger Hammer to the confluence with the Shirebourne spring (Silent Pool), the Tillingbourne valley widens and the "regular, powerful and inexhaustible moving power" of the stream drove a group of old established manorial mills as well as serving tanneries and the piece of distinguished garden-making at Albury. As early as the fourteenth century, watermills working two wheels are encountered in this section of the river and the 'populous and improving locality', which was its characteristic in the first half of the seventeenth century and again in the mid nineteenth century, helps to explain the enlargement of mills and more elaborate machinery at these periods. The most ingenious use of water was the artificial back-flow of spring water from the Shireburn spring eastwards over high ground to supply the fountains at Albury gardens.

Gomshall Mill.

14. Gomshall mill   NGR. TQ085478

Restored timber-framed mill now used as a restaurant. One enclosed wheel in situ.

This disused mill, probably on the site of the Gomshall mill recorded in Domesday Book, was operating until the Second World War. It figures as a manorial corn mill during the middle ages and was extensively rebuilt in 1334. The present building is basically a five-bay, timber-framed structure of at least the early seventeenth century, at which time the mill housed a corn mill and a malt mill under the same roof. During the eighteenth century, the mill was enlarged and for a long period four corn mills were worked. It was thus probably the most important corn milling site in the district. Originally an undershot mill, it was again redesigned in 1839 as an over-shot mill. Hillier records that the smaller of the two wheels was sold for scrap iron at the beginning of the war. Of the larger wheel, he writes: "The remaining wheel is about eighteen feet in diameter and six feet wide. The buckets are so deep that reaching in from the front edge the miller could not touch the bottom with his hands. They are reputed to hold forty gallons apiece, and the thunderous force of this giant as it heaves round under the impetus of the Tillingbourne, cascading from a height of twenty feet through a narrow opening, can be imagined".

In 1884, when the mill was owned by the Kelsey family, it comprised four pairs of stones and modern equipment for crushing oats. In 1902, silk dressing machinery had been additionally installed.

Uniquely in the valley, patrons of the restaurant can enjoy the surviving water-wheel and the mill gearing as an unusual setting to the meal.

Packhorse bridge, Gomshall.

15. Netley mill   NGR. TQ079479

Ornamented mill-pond, bay and pond.

As the name indicates, this mill lay on the demesne of that moiety of Gomshall granted in 1233 to the Abbey of Netley (on the shores of Southampton Water). It was apparently in disuse during the seventeenth century and was entirely rebuilt between 1789 and 1793. The mill is an exception to the purely functional design of the Tillingbourne mills. Its plainness is relieved by decorative features showing the 'Gothic' Picturesque of William Gilpin and Uvedale Price, such as pointed window arches, sills, and square tower and tiled hipped roof.

The mill owes its distinctive architectural features to Edmund Shallett Lomax, an 'improving' landlord of the late eighteenth century. Any suspicion that it was never a working mill is dispelled by a draft lease (written in Lomax's own hand) indicating that Lomax had built the mill at his own expense and had also equipped it with the necessary machinery. He then leased it, retaining a half share of profits. This suggests that his mill was intended to reinforce his role as a manorial proprietor as well as to act as a major landscape feature in his grounds (the ornamented part of the mill would have been clearly visible from his new house of Netley on the hillside above (destroyed by fire in the mid-nineteenth century and subsequently rebuilt). In addition to creating the mill, Lomax strongly defended rights to common land and other manorial perquisites. The older-established landed gentry in the district were rather amused and not a little scornful of Lomax's proud proprietorship but he was able to develop a continuity of ownership and a positive management of an estate. This is now much missed in the Surrey countryside.

The damaging competition of this mill probably led to the eventual closure of the Shere Mill (Site 16).

16. Shere Lower mill   NGR. TQ076478

Pond-bay and weir; workshops on site of mill.

This is a Domesday site. In the fourteenth century, two wheels worked under the same roof.

17. Shere West mill   NGR. TQ067477

Pond-bay; pond; no trace of mill.

Very little is known of this site. It is recorded as a corn mill in a survey of Albury manor dated 1638. The pond has been restored for fish conservation.

Shere village, Lower Street.

18. Albury gardens   NGR. TQ063479

Traces of formal canal-garden.

Albury was the Earl of Arundel's favourite country retreat in the 1630's and one of the earliest examples of the landscape gardener's art. Hollar's skilfully composed etchings of terraced gardens opposite the Earl's 'poore cottage' sloping to the lakeside are brilliantly suggestive of the shimmering light reflected from trees and a 'ruined' casino or grotto on to a wide surface of still water. This sheet of tranquil water had an all-pervading presence in the 'Collector' Earl's nostalgic recollection of Albury during his final years at Padua. These water features were a minimally modified working landscape previously created by the diversion of streams and the building of dams for the purpose of milling and the keeping of fish.

The almost photographic truth of Hollar's drawings of Albury is authenticated by a survey of the Earl's Surrey estate in 1638 which similarly records a chain of ponds stretching from the village of Shere to Old Albury church. Presumably the millponds of mills at sites 17 and 19 are depicted in Hollar's drawings.

Wenceslaus Hollar, *Albury*, c.1670 (based on recollections of the 1630s.)

19. Albury Park mill   NGR. TQ062479

Millhouse; part of site of old village of Albury removed in connection with 19th century landscaping.

A corn mill on this site was destroyed by fire in 1727 following an explosion of gunpowder stored there. It was rebuilt as a corn mill but in 1795 was converted to a paper mill owned by Charles Ball, a leading paper manufacturer, who produced bank notes. The mill closed in the 1820s and by 1844 was in use as a laundry.

The availability of the Tillingbourne for making paper money drew a number of leading banking families to the attractive valley in the early nineteenth century, of which Henry Drummond of Albury is the most famous. For his major contribution to the landscape of Albury and William Cobbett's observations on it, see Peter Brandon, *A History of Surrey*.

20. The Silent Pool   NGR. TQ061484

Spring; Upper and Lower Ponds; culverts; dry leats.

This interesting site was the most fiercely contested natural resource in the valley. Except in the driest of seasons (as in 1741) pure water copiously flowed from the Sherbourne (Shireburn) springs feeding the Upper Pond. Being impregnated with chalk, the water had a fertilizing power to an astonishing degree. In a survey of the Albury estate in 1638, only one pond is recorded. The present lower pond was constructed after that date for the purpose of taking water eastwards i.e. backwards along the valley to supply the fountains at Albury gardens.

These gardens were constructed by John Evelyn for Charles Howard, later Duke of Norfolk in the 1660s, as John Aubrey, in his *History of Surrey,* remarks on the use of

the channelled water in the making of the gardens: "they have command of a spring in this park (the Shireburn) which they bring in a channel to the place where they would have the sand taken away; they dig a convenient part of the sand under which the water is to come and there the water (as it were) dissolves into the sand as you see sugar dissolved in wine..." Evelyn had earlier removed sand at Wotton when laying out his canals and terraced gardens.

A third pond is shown on a map of Albury of 1782. This is now dry. It originated in the complicated dispute between the family of Finch, later lords Aylesford, the owners of Albury house and park, and the Risbridgers, freeholders on the Finchs' estate, and their neighbours, the Duncombes. The Risbridgers' held lands in Weston and also near

Albury church.

the site of Albury Park mill. They and their predecessors alleged that the diversion of water backwards from the Silent Pool deprived them of water for floating their meadows. Like most disputes of this nature, there was disagreement amongst the witnesses. The controversy centred upon the legal right of lords of the manor to divert water from streams. This was never embodied in statute law and was increasingly contested in the seventeenth century. The dispute continued intermittently for over one hundred years and was not finally ended until Lord Aylesford purchased the Risbridger property for the large sum of £1000 in 1749.

Anthony Devis, *Albury Park* (c.1790).
Devis resided for many years in Weston Street.

28

The evidence on the ground is interesting. A culvert from the upper pond is visible at its west end. A dry water channel leading from this is traceable across the footpath below and through the woodland parallel to the highway leading from Shere to Newland's Corner, where it ends in swampy ground on the former site of a large pond clearly shown in a map of 1860. This channel marks an attempt to divert water from the upper pond into water meadows to the south without using the lower pond. This leat can be observed from the Victorian model farm across the main road. The culvert lay on the east side of the lower pond. A dry leat is traceable curving in front of the cottages set back on the north side of the road. It then curves to enter the model farm and can be followed on foot along its course parallel to the road to Albury. A line of trees then marks its course towards Albury gardens. The leat was taken to the point above the central basin. Its survival is not the least significant aspect in which the valley of the Tillingbourne remains in contact with its recognizable past and it is a visible reminder of the period when both landlords and tenants kept constant watch on the level of water and the state of their watercourses.

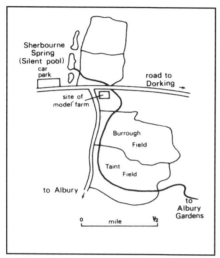

Fountain leat from the Silent Pool.

21. Weston meads   NGR. TQ054481   *Drained pond; mesh of water-channels.*

This floating system is shown on a map of 1782. It is evidently the work of the Duncombes or Risbridgers who sought to provide for a source of water for floating their meadows at a time when they claimed that their rightful source of supply from the Silent Pool had been diverted backwards to Albury Park. The site has been subsequently used for brick-making.

The final stretch of the Tillingbourne from Albury to the point where the river joins the Wey at Shalford was, for long, important for paper and gunpowder manufacture. The origin of the paper-making industry is connected with the West Surrey cloth industry. The earliest paper mills in Surrey produced paper used in pressing cloths and clothmakers supplied the paper-mills with felts for pulping. The growth of the paper industry is also, in part, related to the decline of the cloth industry. The existence of buildings already in use, or which had been converted from water-mills, was a powerful factor in setting up the paper industry. Fulling mills were particularly suitable for conversion because some of their equipment could be employed in paper-making; the hammers, for example, could be used for pounding rags into fibrous pulp or 'stuff' in the preparation of paper.

29

Another control on the siting of paper mills was the purity of water, especially in the production of white paper. The siting of paper mills exclusively below the issue of the Sherbourne spring is probably not accidental for this stretch of the river had the maximum purity of water (A.H. Shorter).

22. Albury mill   NGR. TQ062479   *Late-nineteenth century building converted to use as laboratories.*

This was probably on the site of the mill serving the manor of Weston and is thus an ancient milling site. The old timber-framed building was destroyed by arson in the mid-nineteenth century, the person responsible being hanged. Although of uninteresting appearance, it is an unusual example of a watermill converted from a three-stone mill driven by an overshot wheel to more efficient rollers driven by a turbine. Although this lengthened the working life of the mill, Messrs. Botting and Son moved to larger premises at the newly built mill, on the site of Old Postford mill (site 24) in 1890. It was simply uneconomic for them to continue on a smaller basis with so much keen competition from the large steam-driven mills. The introduction of roller grinding, producing a fine white flour coming into vogue, was an expensive improvement rarely attempted by country millers, whose conservatism itself acted as a brake on change. The accessibility of the railway station of Chilworth may have been a factor in the rise of new plant at Postford.

23. Postford Upper mill   NGR. TQ041480   *No traces apart from Waterloo pond and wheel pit.*

This mill, and its neighbour, Postford Lower mill, were both papermills in the same ownership of Charles Ball at the beginning of the nineteenth century. He appears to have worked this mill directly and his son the other. Both mills ran economically because of the large demand during the Napoleonic Wars for paper and bank notes, but both were difficult to manage successfully with the return to normal trading after 1815. The Upper Mill was disused for a time in the 1830s and finally closed down some years later.

Sited on flat land on the lower course of the Tillingbourne, it was necessary to divert water along a race for a length of nearly one mile from Albury in order to obtain the necessary difference in level between the race and the stream to provide a sufficient head of water. The artificial channel, now largely dry, can be traced without difficulty.

Wenceslaus Hollar, *Albury* (c.1670), showing ornamental buildings removed when Evelyn built the great terrace.

24. Postford Lower mill NGR. TQ039480

Botting's mill, since demolished.

Botting's Mill

Gunpowder mills are shown clustered around Albury (Postford) pond on Seller's map of Surrey, c. 1693.

This site was occupied by C.A.Bottings' corn and animal feed mill and trout farm, until the 1990s, when it was developed for residential use. Owners of the paper mill on this site found it difficult to trade successfully in the 1820s and 1830s with the decline in the issue of bank notes and normal trade in paper. For a time, however, Sir William Magnay, described by the Surrey historian Brayley as 'the principal paper maker of Surrey', was paper-making here in the mid-nineteenth century. He sold both the Upper and Lower mills in 1865 and the Lower mill appears to have closed for paper making in 1876.

Hand paper making

25,26,27. Chilworth upper NGR.TQ039480
lower NGR.TQ025475
middle NGR.TQ028475

Many visible remains of gunpowder manu-facture; site of paper mill

These are particularly fascinating sites for the industrial archaeologist for they record nearly three hundred years of gunpowder making.

The lower site, adjacent to Chilworth manor which was landscaped by the Randalls in the mid-seventeenth century, first came into prominence as a corn and fulling-mill centre owned by the monks of Syon Abbey. After the Reformation, it became one of the most famous industrial sites in England. About 1600, Thomas Le Steere of Wotton and Ockley enticed hammermen, smiths and tool-makers to leave the then sole existing brass manufactory at Tintern, Gwent, in defiance of the monopoly of the Mineral and Battery Company. The site again comes to notice as that of a gunpowder works operated by the East India Company between 1626-36. The Company's ill-starred operations were marked by several explosions and by the flooding of hop grounds and fields through defects at the pond-heads. The new premises erected by Samuel Cordwell and George Collins extended, apparently , on to the middle site, and it is possible that Morgan Randall's eighteen powder mills noted (c. 1675) by John Aubrey in his *History of Surrey* included some on the upper site, now represented by Postford pond. These are shown on Seller's map of Surrey (c.1693). Glenys Crocker has suggested that these works were simple pestle mills operated by a water wheel raising hammers by means of a cam shaft. (*A short history of the Chilworth gunpowder works*, Surrey Industrial History Group.) Gunpowder continued to be made at Chilworth until 1920 and the works in the closing stages were especially concerned with the production and development of smokeless powder and cordite.

The main focus of visual interest lies in the now public open space between Blacksmith and Lockner Farm Lanes. Of the water features, the mill-stream on the extreme south of the site and the water channels dropping down to power the incorporating mills used for mixing powder are conspicuous. Also traceable at a number of sites is the track of a mineral railway used to transport coal when the incorporating mills had been converted to steam power. This track crosses the mill-stream by a swing-bridge and its course can be followed to Chilworth railway station by means of a footpath. Along the banks of the millstream are numerous incorporating mill-stones. The little buildings at the rear of the incorporating mills were engine houses (R.J.Puddick, *Chilworth gunpowder works*). The modern buildings towards Lockner Lane include many magazines. The site of the black corning house which exploded with six fatalities in 1901 was possibly adjacent to a cottage used by the timekeeper.

Water-power channel, Chilworth gunpowder works (middle site).

At the site of the conspicuous spill-way on Blacksmith Lane was a paper-mill shown on Senex's map of Surrey, 1729. When destroyed by fire at the end of the nineteenth century, it was owned by Unwins, the famous printers.

28 Shalford mill   NGR. TQ001478

Eighteenth century timber-framed building astride the river.

Although disused since 1914, Shalford mill is the best preserved of all the mills that were once worked by the Tillingbourne, thanks to a local group of preservationists know as Ferguson's Gang who raised money to buy, restore and to endow it as a possession of the National Trust in 1932. (Robin Fedden, *The continuing purpose* (1966), pp. 32-3.) A mill has stood on this site since before 1086 and in its present form is a delightful eighteenth-century timber-framed building with brick walls to first floor height and tile-hung walls above. A unique feature is the large over-hanging storey with its sack hoist. The mill-pond occupied the site of the field to the south of the mill. By the footpath leading to the field can be seen the sluice taking water from the river to supply the next mill down stream.

The top half of the low-breast-shot waterwheel, 14ft. in diameter and 7ft.6in. wide is still *in situ*. There are four floors. The equipment on the ground floor, where the meal was collected into bins and sacks, retains its iron pit wheel transmitting power to the great spur wheel which drove three pairs of stones on the floor above. Here, one pair of stones is intact, the bedstones of the other two pairs also remaining. On the second floor is the auxiliary machinery of the mill which worked the sack hoist and oat crusher, also worked with water power by means of a large crown wheel which is intact. The sack hoist delivered grain to large storage bins which can be seen on the third floor, projecting on pillars above the waterwheel. (F.G.Gregory, *Guide to Shalford mill*) (National Trust).

Interior of Shalford mill.

THE OVERALL SCENIC EFFECT OF MILLING IN THE VALLEY

Milling has created one of the most characteristic forms of rural settlement in Surrey, the mill hamlet. Within the district under survey are numerous examples of this type, including Friday Street, Abinger Bottom, Abinger Hammer, Broadmoor, Sutton and Pitland Street. Each of these settlements was in the setting of at least one water-mill and directly related to it for employment. They are interesting in a number of ways. They are criss-crossed with defunct leats and flood-water channels; they contain a 'mill farm', numerous drained ponds and traces of spillways. The fields around them are of 'assart' type, small, patchwork closes. Each mill-hamlet is predominantly built in the architectural style of the early seventeenth century which in central Surrey was typically half-timbered 'mud' dwellings (brick-nogged subsequently) or stone buildings.

From documentary sources it is sometimes possible to date fairly precisely the origin of the mill-hamlets. Broadmoor is described as 'six newly erected cottages, enclosure and a mill' in c.1607; Friday Street in 1612 as 'three cottages, a new mill, millhouse, wheels, millstones lately erected on Wotton Common together with floodgate, sluice and millponds'; Pitland Street as 'cottages and mill, millhouse and ponds' in 1623; Abinger Hammer as 'Shere hammer lately erected, with barns, millhouses, closes and cottages for the iron men' in 1564.

B.W. Leader, R.A., *Burrow's Cross*, Gomshall (c.1920). Woodland cleared for the milling industries. Replaced by windswept pineland.

It was not only the valley scenery which was changed by the water-milling but also the hillsides and the hill tops. South of the Dorking to Guildford road these were largely tree covered in the early sixteenth-century. Extensive acreages were common-woods, including the Manwood, over 1,000 acres and the Churt (Hurt) Wood, over 2,000 acres. It was the availability of considerable reserves of timber (although thinly grown), as well as water-power potential, that made the manors of Wotton, Abinger, Paddington and Shere so attractive to the industrialist. By the early seventeenth century large tracts of the common woodland had been forcibly enclosed and were the subject of litigation. Clear felling was widespread and regeneration of trees effectively hindered by the lack of control over grazing animals. Evelyn himself speaks of the devastation in *The Sylva* (1664) as 'epidemical'.

The demand for wood fuel to support the charcoal iron industry and to a lesser extent the gunpowder, brass and copper industries, together with the expanding population both in London and its surrounding countryside had made serious inroads into fuel supplies. The limited timber stocks on the commons were butchered and this destructive action profoundly altered the appearance of the landscape, in some places permanently. The naked look of the Surrey heaths so familiar to Defoe and Cobbett were in fact scars which could not be healed on the light, porous soils. In these districts even the wood fuel the peasant had traditionally used became scarce and the back-breaking task of winning peat or turves was a necessary replacement. At several places the sites of peat moors can be located.

It is not stretching the evidence too far in calling the west Surrey commons a devastated terrain. Not until self-sown Scots Pine seeded itself in great quantities during the

eighteenth and early nineteenth centuries was the heathland again partially covered with trees. The degeneration in the appearance of the valley of the Tillingbourne in the sixteenth and seventeenth centuries thus points to an early example of the imbalance between the evolution of man's technology and his destruction of long-lasting and well-adapted life ways.

Peat-drying (from E. Bowen's map of the county of Surrey) (1753).

A tabulation of data from the

DOMESDAY BOOK – 1086

MANOR

WOTTON	: A Mill at 20d.
SUTTON	: –
ABINGER	: A Mill at 6s.
PADDINGTON	: A Mill at 6s.
GOMSHALL	: A Mill at 40d.
SHERE	: 2 Mills at 10s.
ALBURY	: A Mill at 5s
CHILWORTH	: A Mill at 7s.
SHALFORD	: 3 Mills at 16s.